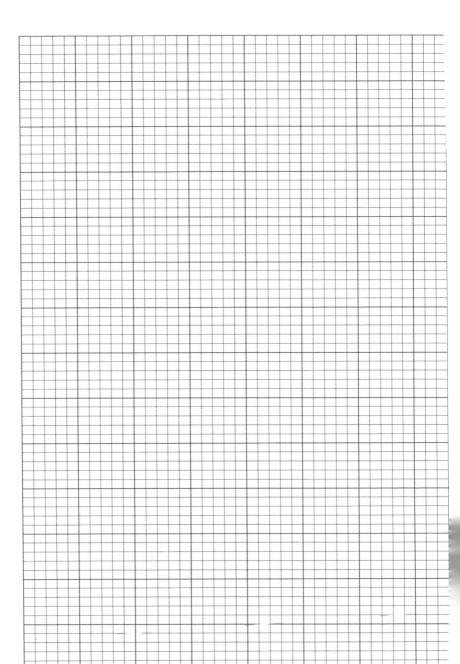

Skill Set

Beginning Knitting

Kay Gardiner and
Ann Shayne

Contents

4. **INTRODUCTION**
   Welcome

6. **LESSON 1**
   Supplies, Casting On,
   Knit Stitch, Binding Off

21. **LESSON 2**
    Purl Stitch, Combining
    Knits and Purls

29. **LESSON 3**
    Basic Shaping:
    Increases and Decreases

35.	**LESSON 4** Knitting in the Round	79.	**LESSON 8** Patterns, Yarn, and Gear
47.	**LESSON 5** Basic Lace and Cables	97.	**LESSON 9** Fixing Mistakes
55.	**LESSON 6** Basic Colorwork: Stripes, Stranding, Intarsia	106.	**CONCLUSION** What We Haven't Taught You
69.	**LESSON 7** Finishing: Weaving in Ends, Seaming, Blocking		

Welcome

Loops on a stick, one pulled through the other. That's all there is to knitting.

The simplicity of this action is elegant, clever, endlessly new. With it we can make fabric and give it purpose: a small square is a dishcloth; a big rectangle is a scarf, a shawl, or a blanket; a tube is a cowl, a sleeve, the body of a sweater, or a sock. And on and on.

Skill Set: Beginning Knitting presents everything you need to know to start knitting—and nothing you don't need. We have divided the basics into 9 short lessons, and we have done our best to keep each lesson simple. It may seem surprising, but with the elementary techniques presented in Lesson 1, you can knit for a lifetime. Or you can work your way through Lesson 9, then keep going and explore for the rest of your life. There's always something interesting to discover whenever you decide you are ready for a new challenge.

Between the two of us, we have been knitting for more than 40 years. We met and became friends through knitting. Knitting has taken us all over the country, introduced us to countless wonderful people, and broadened our thinking. Knitting has also given us the chance to make piles of blankets, sweaters, hats, and scarves (and so much more)—for ourselves and for all the willing family and friends around us.

This book is your passport to the fun that awaits.

We made *Skill Set* small so that you can always have it with you. Someday soon, you will feel so confident that you won't need it anymore; on that day, we hope you'll pass it on to another new knitter.

Let's get started. Not a minute to waste!

Kay   Ann

LESSON 1

Supplies, Casting On, Knit Stitch, Binding Off

To knit, you need needles and yarn. That's all. No electricity, no bicycle pump, no outbuilding for equipment. It's as simple as singing a song—though, as we all know, once somebody goes all in on something, that's how we end up with *Bohemian Rhapsody*.

Gather Supplies

We are firm believers in the motto "Love your gear," and it is an understatement to say that we enjoy the shopping that comes with a full-blown knitting obsession. But for the moment, you need very little indeed.

A pair of needles. To start, we like 10" (25 cm) long straight needles. Wood or metal, your choice. Size US 8 (5mm).

Yarn. Worsted-weight wool is good, sturdy stuff. Get two balls in different colors.

NEEDLE BASICS

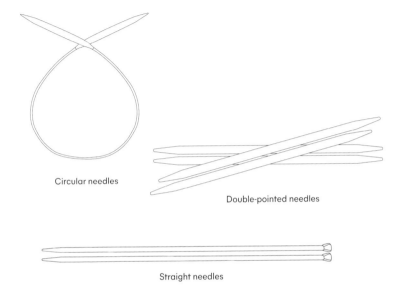

Circular needles

Double-pointed needles

Straight needles

There are three main categories of knitting needles. Straight needles look like dowels with a stopper on one end. Double-pointed needles are similar to straight needles, but they have points on both ends. Circular needles look like two short, pointed dowels with a cord connecting them.

Needles come in a range of diameters. A size US 1 (2.5 mm) needle is very small, and a size US 15 (10 mm) needle is much larger.

YARN BASICS

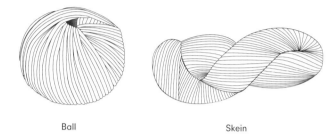

Ball   Skein

Yarn comes in many different thicknesses, or weights. Worsted-weight, which we recommend for beginners, is average, not too thin and not too thick. It is widely available and easy to knit with.

Yarn can be made out of all sorts of fibers, such as wool, acrylic, cotton, and linen. Yarn is sold in balls that you can work from directly and in skeins (which look like figure-eights) that need to be untwisted and then wound into balls.

We encourage you to work with natural fibers rather than acrylics, because they feel great to wear, knit up beautifully, and are often gentler on the environment. Don't think it's not worth it to use the good stuff because you're just starting out. When you consider the amount of time you will be spending with yarn as you knit, the cost per hour is low.

WINDING YARN INTO A BALL

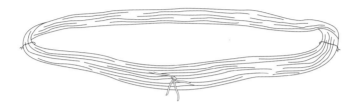

If your yarn is in skein form, you will need to wind it into a ball before you knit from it, as follows:

Untwist the figure-eight so that it is one big loop. Cut any short strands of yarn or string that are tied or wrapped around the yarn. Look for the two ends of the yarn; if they are tied together, cut or untie them. If you are working alone, place the loop of yarn on the back of a chair or around your knees while sitting cross-legged. If you have a helper, place the loop over their arms.

Take one end and begin winding the yarn loosely around the fingers of your other hand. When a small ball begins to form, slip out your fingers. Continue winding, rotating the ball as you go, being careful not to put any tension on the yarn as you wind.

Casting On

Each row of knitting is a row of loops that are pulled through the loops of the row below. To begin a project, you place a specified number of loops (stitches) on the needle. This is called casting on. There are many different ways to cast on and someday you might want to investigate them. For now, we're going to set you up with the long-tail cast-on, which is elastic and versatile. We rarely use any other cast-on despite knowing a bunch of other methods.

STARTING WITH A SLIPKNOT

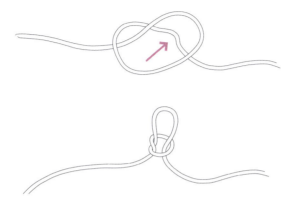

The long-tail cast-on begins with a slipknot (as do most cast-ons). We'd like you to make a slipknot 30" (76 cm) from the end of the yarn.

At the 30" (76 cm) point, make a circle with the yarn. Move the yarn on top to the back of the circle and pull that yarn through the circle to make a loop. Put the loop on your needle, and pull on both strands to snug up the slipknot. There it is! Your first stitch!

Now, turn the page to learn how to cast on more stitches.

LONG-TAIL CAST-ON

This cast-on uses 2 strands of yarn: the end of the ball of yarn, called the tail, and the working yarn, aka the rest of the ball of yarn. Keep the tail in front and working yarn in back as you go.

1. Hold the needle with the slipknot in your right hand. Hold both ends of the yarn in the fingers of your left hand. Bring your left thumb and forefinger between the strands, opening them up to form a diamond.

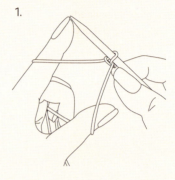

2. Rotate your hand slightly up and to the left, still holding both strands with the left three fingers.

3. Point the tip of the needle at the base of the left thumb. Slide the needle up and through the front (thumb) loop.

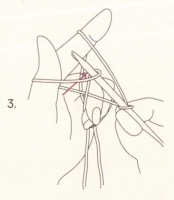

4. Swing the needle to the right, moving it over the index finger strand.

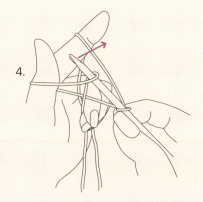

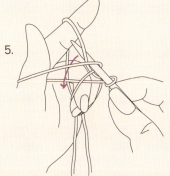

5. Move the index finger strand back through the thumb loop. Remove your thumb, snug up gently.

Repeat Steps 1–5 until you have 30 stitches.

Congratulations! This is the fanciest part of learning to knit, and you only have to do it once for each piece you knit. The next part is where you'll get your groove going.

Knit Stitch

The knit stitch is the mother stitch from which all knitting—from dishcloths to lace wedding veils—flows. With repetition, the simple movements of forming a knit stitch—in, around, through, and off—will become so familiar that you will be able to do them with your eyes closed.

KNITTING THE FIRST ROW

1. IN: Place needle with cast-on stitches in your left hand. Insert the right needle into the left side of the front of the first stitch on the left needle. Use a light pincer grip with your left thumb and index finger (or your right thumb and index finger) to keep the needles stable.

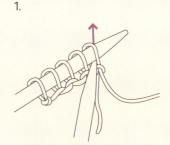

2. AROUND: With the working yarn behind the right needle, make a loop around the right needle, by wrapping the yarn around the needle, back to front between the needles.

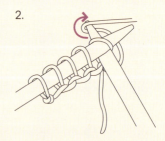

3. THROUGH: Pull the working yarn through the stitch on the left needle and to the front of the work.

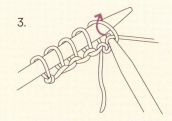

4. OFF: Pull the stitch on the left needle off the left needle. You now have a brand-new stitch on the right needle.

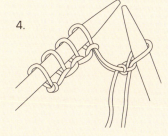

Now: Practice. Knit all the stitches in the row. Repeat to yourself, "in, around, through, off," as you make each stitch.

Your first row of knitting is complete! All the new stitches are now on the right needle.

KNITTING THE SECOND AND SUBSEQUENT ROWS

To knit the next row, put the needle that holds all your new stitches in your left hand, and position it so that the tip points to the right. Something to notice: the stitches that you just completed are now old stitches. You are going to repeat the process by pulling a loop through each of the stitches on the left needle and transferring it to the right needle.

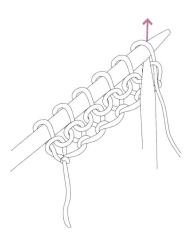

Before you start each new row of stitches, do this check: look at the stitches on the left needle to make sure the yarn is coming out of the bottom of the first stitch as shown. If it's not, simply put the yarn in that position.

Now, you get to practice. Knit a row, then another and another. At the beginning of each row, check the illustration to make sure that your needle is entering that first stitch the correct way.

Keep at it until your piece of knitting looks approximately square in shape. This should take 60 rows or so, but don't worry about counting rows right now. We'll cover that later.

When you knit every stitch in every row, you are doing what knitters call garter stitch. The fabric you create is referred to as garter stitch as well.

Binding Off

While you were knitting, you may have been wondering, how will I get this piece of knitting off the needle without it unraveling? You will do that with a technique called binding off. Start the bind-off row by knitting 2 stitches. You now have 2 stitches on the right needle.

1. With the left needle, lift the first stitch over the second stitch on the right needle and drop it off the needle. Now you're back to just 1 stitch on the right needle. You've bound off 1 stitch.

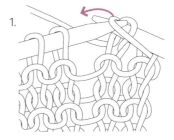

2. Knit 1 stitch.

Repeat Steps 1 and 2 across the row—until there is 1 stitch left on the right needle. Now cut the working yarn, leaving 4" (10 cm) of tail. Pull the tail through that last stitch.

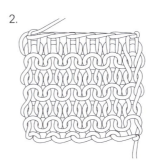

> What if my knitting looks wonky? Trust us: this problem, if you have it, will go away all by itself. Just keep knitting. Hold the needles lightly. Pull the yarn gently. A relaxed rhythm takes a little time to develop, but it will make your stitches even.

Joining a New Yarn

You will need to join a new yarn whenever you run out of your current yarn or if you want to change from one yarn to another yarn (for example, from one color to another).

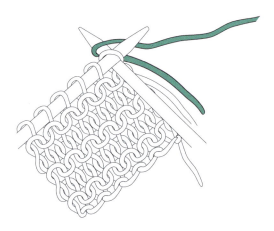

Join a new yarn at an edge when you're ready to begin a new row. Drop the old yarn. Holding the yarn snugly in your right hand, knit the first stitch with the new yarn, leaving a 4" (10 cm) tail, then continue knitting with the new yarn.

LESSON 2

Purl Stitch, Combining Knits and Purls

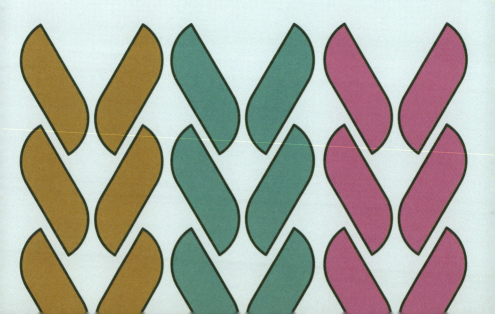

Like the knit stitch, the purl stitch is a simple matter of drawing a loop of yarn through the loop on the needle—with two differences:

- You start with the yarn in the front instead of the back of the work.

- Your right needle enters the loop on the needle from the right instead of the left.

You can say the same four words to yourself as you work purl stitches: in, around, through, and off.

1. IN: Begin with the working yarn in front of your work. Insert the right needle into the right side of the front of the first stitch on the left needle.

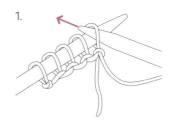

2. AROUND: With the working yarn in front of the right needle, make a loop counterclockwise around the right needle.

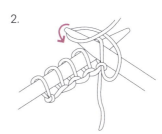

3. THROUGH: Pull the working yarn backwards through the stitch on the left needle.

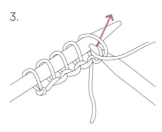

4. OFF: Pull the stitch on the left needle off the left needle. You now have a brand-new stitch on the right needle, and it's a purl stitch.

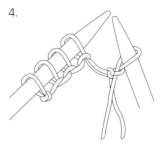

Knit and Purl Stitches

Knits and purls are a symbiotic match, complete on their own and mutually beneficial when together. By combining them in different ways, a whole world of texture opens up. In some cases, the fabric produced is basically the same on both sides. And, in other cases, the two sides are different: one is referred to as the right side, and the other is referred to as the wrong side. If both sides are equally presentable, the fabric is described as reversible.

In Lesson 1, you learned the term *garter stitch* for a fabric created by working only the knit stitch on every row. Let's look at some really common ways to combine knits and purls. These patterns are instantly recognizable to all knitters. Soon you will recognize them, too. Start looking at strangers' sweaters (which is something knitters do)—these are the stitch patterns you will see most often.

GARTER STITCH

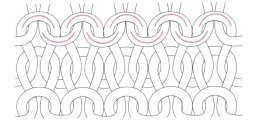

Knit every row. The bumpy fabric you create looks the same on both sides. Note how two rows interlock into a ridge of "smiles and frowns"—U shapes and upside-down U shapes.

STOCKINETTE STITCH

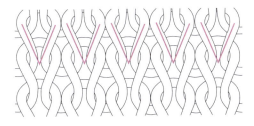

Knit a row, then purl a row. Keep alternating knit and purl rows. The knit side looks flat, and the purl side looks bumpy. Typically, the flat side is considered the right, or public, side. When the purl side is presented as the right side, it is called reverse stockinette stitch. Note how the stitches on the flat side resemble V shapes.

RIBBING

2 × 2 ribbing

Alternate a specific number of knits and purls across the row. Knit X stitches, then purl X stitches. Two very common ribbing patterns are 1 × 1 ribbing and 2 × 2 ribbing (shown). Both are reversible (meaning they look basically the same on both sides).

1 × 1 ribbing: Cast on an even number of stitches. Knit 1 stitch, then purl 1 stitch. Keep alternating knit stitches and purl stitches. Repeat this for a few rows.

2 × 2 ribbing: Cast on a multiple of 4 stitches. Knit 2 stitches, then purl 2 stitches. Keep alternating 2 knits and 2 purls. Repeat this for a few rows.

Note: To combine knits and purls in the same row, simply move the yarn between the needles to the appropriate position: behind the needles if the next stitch will be a knit stitch, and in front of the needles if the next stitch will be a purl stitch.

Practice Reading Your Knitting

Once you start combining knits and purls, you will want to be able to identify them on your needles and in your fabric. That way, if you put your knitting down in the middle of the row, when you pick it back up again, you'll know what the next stitch should be.

To practice reading your knitting, cast on 32 stitches. Knit 10 rows. Work 10 rows of knit 2/purl 2. Knit 10 rows. Work 10 rows of knit 2/purl 2. Keep at this until you have a square. Bind off.

See the way the knit stitches in the ribbing are V shaped? And how the purl stitches are bumpy little pearls? You're reading your knitting.

Stitch Mount

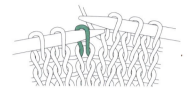
Properly mounted

Twisted

Similar to the way you sit on a horse, a stitch sits on your needle. The right "leg" of the stitch appears in front of your work, and the left "leg" is behind it. Stitches can end up mounted wrong on the needle when you've unknit and replaced stitches on the needle. Or it can happen when you're fixing dropped stitches.

The illustration on the left shows a properly mounted stitch. When you insert a needle as if to knit, the stitch opens up.

The illustration on the right shows an improperly mounted stitch. When you insert a needle as if to knit, the stitch doesn't open up. It's twisted.

To fix an improperly mounted stitch, simply lift the stitch off the needle, turn it so that the legs swap positions, and replace it on the needle.

Later you'll discover cool stitch patterns that require a stitch mount to change. But as you're getting started, you'll want all your stitches to sit the same way.

LESSON 3

Basic Shaping: Increases and Decreases

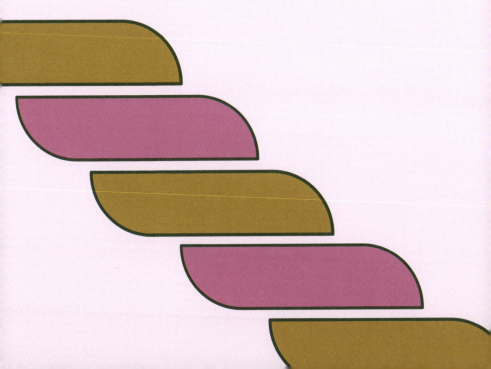

You can have a rich and rewarding knitting life working with only knit and purl stitches. If you are a fan of scarves and blankets—basically, anything square or rectangular—then knit and purl are all you need to know. However, new possibilities emerge when you start adding stitches to or subtracting stitches from your row. All of a sudden, you can make a sleeve, a curve on a shawl, the toe of a sock.

Increasing

An increase adds a stitch to a row. The simplest of increases is the knit-front-and-back stitch. You knit into the front of the stitch, as usual, but you leave the stitch on the left needle. Then insert the right needle through the back of the same stitch, knit it, then pull the completed knit-front-and-back stitch (now 2 stitches instead of the 1 stitch you started with) off the left needle. In the language of knitting, this increase is abbreviated as kfb.

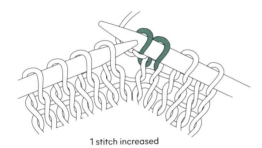

1 stitch increased

Decreasing

A decrease subtracts a stitch from a row. The simplest decrease is called knit 2 together, and it's as simple as it sounds. Insert your right needle up into the left side of the second stitch on the left needle, then into the first stitch on the left needle. Knit them together and all of a sudden, you have 1 less stitch on this row. In the language of knitting, this decrease is abbreviated as k2tog.

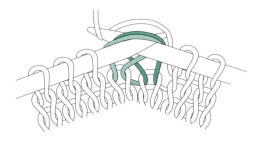

Insert right needle into 2 stitches at the same time

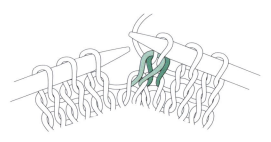

1 stitch decreased

Practicing Increasing and Decreasing

In this practice piece, you'll see what happens when you repeat increases or decreases in an organized way. You'll also knit a small version of a dishcloth known as "Grandma's Favorite."

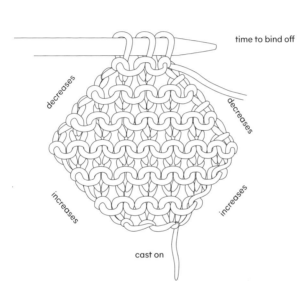

Cast on 3 stitches.

Row 1: Kfb, knit to the end of the row. (1 stitch increased)

Repeat Row 1 on every row until—as if by magic—you have 20 stitches on your needles. See how it grows?

(pattern continues on next page)

Row 2: K2tog, knit to the end of the row. (1 stitch decreased)

Repeat Row 2 until you have only 3 stitches left on your needles. Bind off.

Looked at from cast-on to bind-off, you have made a diamond that is formed of two triangles, one made by increasing 1 stitch at the beginning of every row, and one made by decreasing 1 stitch at the beginning of every row. The diamond has 4 equal sides.

Looked at from edge to edge, it's a square, but the rows of knitting appear to slant. This is called knitting on the bias, which is sometimes done on purpose to enhance the drape and stretch of the fabric.

LESSON 4

Knitting in the Round

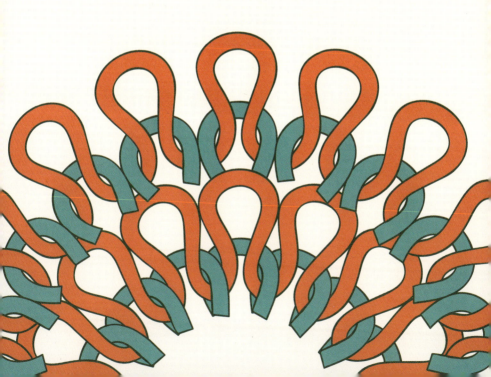

So far, you've been knitting back and forth on 2 straight needles, which creates flat pieces of fabric. Now we're going to show you how to knit a tube on a circular needle (2 needles connected by a cord) and on a set of 4 double-pointed needles.

Knowing how to knit in the round will set you up for all sorts of glory. The tube is the basic form of so many things: socks, sweaters, hats, and mittens, for starters.

Working in the Round with a Circular Needle

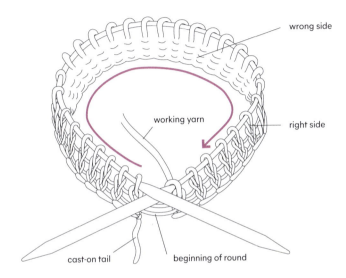

When working in the round, the stitches travel from one needle to the cable to the other needle in a circular form. You work stitches in a spiral of continuous rounds to create a fabric tube. The right side is on the outside of the tube, and the wrong side is on the inside of the tube.

The only new skill you need to learn is how to set up to start knitting in the round, which is called "joining to work in the round."

JOINING TO WORK IN THE ROUND

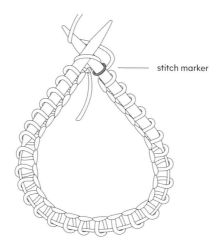

stitch marker

To get started, cast on the required number of stitches using a circular needle.

1. Form a circle with the needles, with the last stitch you cast on, on the right needle, with the working yarn coming from it. Place a stitch marker (see page 95) on the right needle to mark the beginning of the round.

2. Knit the first stitch you cast on. Notice: the working yarn crosses over the marker. This crossing over is the "join"—it creates the tube. Every time you finish a round, slip the marker from the left needle to the right needle. You will remove it when you're finished!

JOINING WITHOUT TWISTING STITCHES

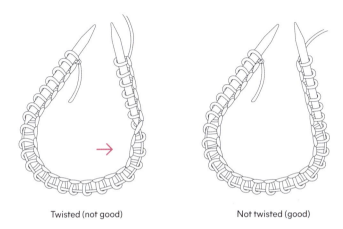

Twisted (not good)   Not twisted (good)

There's a common warning in knitting patterns: After casting on stitches, "Join to knit in the round, being careful not to twist the stitches." This admonition has reminded us many times to double-check the alignment of stitches on the needle. If the cast-on is twisted, and the twist is not corrected before you knit the second round, it can't be corrected; as the piece grows, you will eventually realize that it's irreversibly twisted, and you'll have to start over.

The way to avoid this dire fate is simple. After casting on, lay the needle on a flat surface. Check the circle of stitches for twists—the basic idea is that the cast-on edge should land on one side of the cable, all the way around.

CHOOSING THE CORRECT CORD LENGTH

1. The pattern should tell you the length of circular needle to use. If the number of stitches on your needles will increase or decrease as you work the pattern, you may need to switch to a different circular needle length; the pattern should tell you this also.

2. The principle is that the needle should be long enough to hold the circle of stitches without spreading them out too far, which would make the stitches challenging (if not impossible) to knit. A circular needle that is a little too short is preferable to one that is a little too long.

USING CIRCULAR NEEDLES TO KNIT BACK AND FORTH

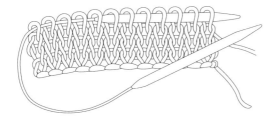

In addition to using circular needles to knit in the round, you can also use them to knit back and forth (like you do with straight needles). This is necessary when you have a large number of stitches, more than can comfortably fit on your longest straight needles. Many knitters use circular needles exclusively, preferring them no matter the number of stitches.

> We encourage you to try circular needles as soon as possible. The benefits:
>
> - Easy to manage.
> - Harder to lose in sofa cushions.
> - Less weight on hands and wrists than straight needles, because the knitted fabric rests in your lap.
> - Can be used when knitting flat or knitting in the round.

Knitting in the Round on Double-Pointed Needles

When you want to knit a tube that is too narrow for a circular needle—the top of a hat, the cuff of a sleeve—double-pointed needles (abbreviated as dpns) are the answer. They require some practice, but you'll find your rhythm soon enough.

GETTING STARTED WITH DOUBLE-POINTED NEEDLES

1. Gather a set of 4 dpns and cast on all stitches required onto one. Next, slide roughly a third of the stitches onto a second dpn, and the remaining stitches onto a third dpn. Form the 3 needles into a triangle, with the working yarn on the right needle. Mark the beginning of the round with a locking stitch marker on the first stitch. Make sure not to twist the stitches before joining (see page 39).

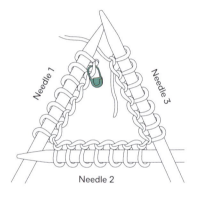

Ready to begin working stitches on Needle 1

You'll be knitting the stitches in the round, from one dpn to the next. There's always a fourth dpn that is the action needle—the one used to do the knitting, held in the right hand.

2. Hold the fourth dpn in your right hand and the first dpn with stitches on it in your left. Knit those stitches, which moves them from the left needle to the right. When all stitches from Needle 1 are on the needle in your right hand, the left needle will be empty. That newly empty needle now becomes the needle to knit with—move it to your right hand.

Now knit the Needle 2 stitches. Pull firmly on the first 2 stitches to avoid loose stitches between the needles; this is called laddering. This takes some practice. When all stitches from Needle 2 are on the right needle, the left needle will be empty. That newly empty needle now becomes the needle to knit with—move it to your right hand.

3. Knit the Needle 3 stitches. At the end, you'll be back at the start of the round. Remember to pull snugly when starting a new dpn.

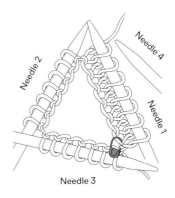

Ready to begin working stitches on Needle 2

Practicing Knitting in the Round and Making a Hat While You're At It

Up until now, we've suggested that you make swatches to practice the skills we are introducing here. Now we're encouraging you to make a hat to practice circular knitting. This basic rolled-brim style covers everything: how to cast on and join stitches in the round to start the brim and how to switch to double-pointed needles as you decrease stitches for the crown.

This adult-sized hat will be about 20.5" (52 cm) circumference, 10.75" (27.5 cm) high with brim unrolled. Depending on how tightly or loosely you knit, you may get a smaller or larger hat, but the point here is to learn how to knit in the round. You'll fine-tune sizing later.

You'll need:
Approximately 135 yards (124 meters) worsted-weight yarn
Size US 8 (5 mm) circular needle, 16" (40 cm) long
Size US 8 (5 mm) double-pointed needles (dpns)
Locking stitch marker
Tapestry needle

Using your circular needle, cast on 92 stitches. Join to work in the round, being careful not to twist the stitches. Place a locking stitch marker on the first stitch of the first round. Begin stockinette stitch (knit every round) and work until piece measures about 7.25" (18.5 cm) from the cast-on edge.

SHAPE CROWN

Change to dpns. To do this, at the start of the round, knit 30 stitches from your circular needle onto your first dpn; now knit the next 30 stitches onto your second dpn; and, finally, the remaining 32 stitches onto your third dpn. Set aside your circular needle. Place the locking stitch marker on the first stitch on the first dpn. Begin working the next round with your action needle (the 4th dpn).

(pattern continues on next page)

Decrease Round 1: *Knit 2 stitches together, knit 44; repeat from * once more—90 stitches remain.

Knit 1 round.

Decrease Round 2: *Knit 2 stitches together, knit 3; repeat from * to the end—72 stitches remain.

Knit 5 rounds.

Decrease Round 3: *Knit 2 stitches together, knit 2; repeat from * to the end—54 stitches remain.

Knit 5 rounds.

Decrease Round 4: *Knit 2 stitches together, knit 1; repeat from * to the end—36 stitches remain.

Knit 3 rounds.

Decrease Round 5: *Knit 2 stitches together; repeat from * to the end—18 stitches remain.

Knit 1 round.

Decrease Round 6: *Knit 2 stitches together; repeat from * to the end—9 stitches remain.

Cut yarn, leaving an 8" (20.5 cm) tail. Thread the tail onto a tapestry needle and pass the needle through the remaining stitches once, removing the stitches from the needles as you go. Then take the tail to the inside of the hat to secure it.

Weave in the ends (see page 71). Put your hat on your head!

LESSON 5

Basic Lace and Cables

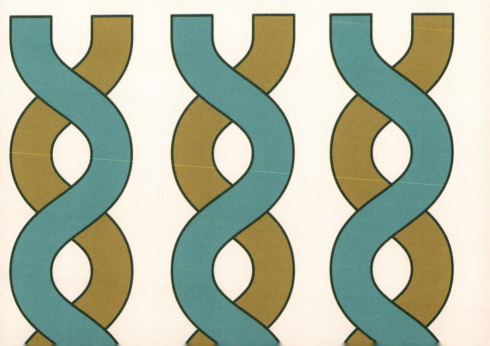

Lace and cables share these exciting characteristics: they're simple techniques that pack a huge punch and can be elaborated upon endlessly. We'll show you the basics here, then set you off on what can easily become a lifetime of new discoveries.

Lace

When it comes down to it, lace is just a bunch of holes presented in an orderly fashion. Amazingly, to make a lifetime of lace projects, all you need to add to your repertoire is a simple workhorse stitch: the yarnover.

WORKING A YARNOVER

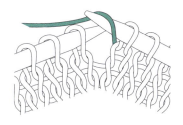

Yo between 2 knit stitches
(ready to work next stitch)

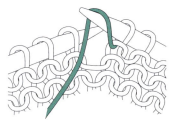

Yo between 2 purl stitches
(ready to work next stitch)

The yarnover (abbreviated as yo in patterns) is simply a matter of carrying the working yarn over the right-hand needle, so that once you work your next stitch, an intentional hole is formed. It increases the stitch count by one. If you keep doing yarnovers, your piece will quickly grow. If you want your stitch count to remain the same, you pair each yarnover with a decrease.

WORKING YARNOVERS ON THE NEXT ROW

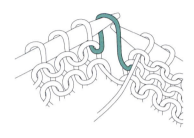

Yo on reverse side of
stockinette stitch

If there's anything tricky about yarnovers, it's making sure you don't drop them off the needle in the subsequent row. Be sure to pay close attention as you make your way through the stitches. When in doubt, recount your stitches at the end of the row or even as you go while you are learning.

When you come to the yarnover on the wrong side, purl it.

PRACTICING YARNOVERS: MAKING EYELETS

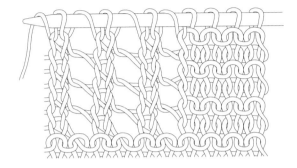

For this practice swatch, you make holes evenly spaced across the right-side rows. In the language of knitting, those holes are called eyelets.

Using a pair of size US 8 (5 mm) straight needles and worsted-weight yarn, cast on 30 stitches.

Knit 4 rows to create a good bottom border.

Row 1 (right side): Knit 4, *yarnover, knit 2 together; repeat from the * to the last 4 stitches, then knit those 4 stitches.

Row 2 (wrong side): Knit 4, purl to the last 4 stitches (including the yarnovers), then knit those 4 stitches.

Repeat Rows 1 and 2 until you're feeling confident.

Knit 4 more rows to even out your swatch, then bind off.

Cables

Cables are ropelike twists in knitted fabric. Making them requires changing the order of stitches on your needle, so one set of stitches crosses over or under another set of stitches. This is typically done with the help of a cable needle. We're going to start with a swatch featuring a basic 2 × 2 cable, which involves two sets of 2 stitches crossing each other.

LEFT-TWISTING 2 × 2 CABLE

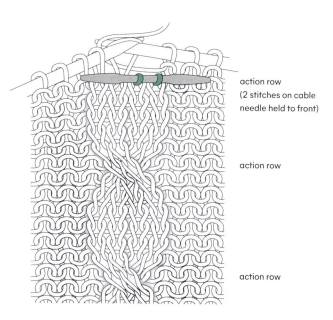

action row
(2 stitches on cable
needle held to front)

action row

action row

PRACTICING CABLES

Using size US 8 (5 mm) needles and worsted-weight yarn, cast on 36 stitches. Locate your cable needle (see page 96).

Row 1 (right side): Knit 4, *purl 4, knit 4; repeat from the * to the end.

Row 2 (wrong side): Knit 8, *purl 4, knit 4; repeat from the * to the last 4 stitches, knit 4.

Row 3: Repeat Row 1.

Row 4: Repeat Row 2.

Row 5: (this is the action row, where you twist the cables): Knit 4, purl 4, then slip 2 stitches onto the cable needle.

With the stitches on the cable needle held to the front of the work, knit the next 2 stitches from the left needle (see left).

Knit the 2 held stitches straight off of the cable needle. That's it. You've twisted the cable to the left. Next, purl 4, make a second cable as above, purl 4, make a third cable, purl 4, knit 4.

Row 6: Repeat Row 2.

Rows 7–18: Repeat Rows 1–6 twice more.

Rows 19–22: Repeat Rows 1–4.

RIGHT-TWISTING 2 × 2 CABLE

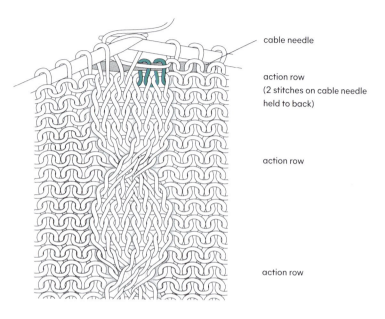

cable needle

action row
(2 stitches on cable needle held to back)

action row

action row

Now try out right-twisting cables.

Follow the instructions for the swatch you just made to learn left-twisting cables. Every row is the same except for Row 5 (the action row, where you twist the cables), which now reads:

Row 5: Knit 4, purl 4, then slip 2 stitches onto the cable needle. With the stitches on the cable needle held to the back of the work, knit the next 2 stitches from the left needle. Knit the 2 held stitches straight off the cable needle. To finish the row, purl 4, make a second cable as above, purl 4, make a third cable, purl 4, knit 4.

LESSON 6

Basic Colorwork

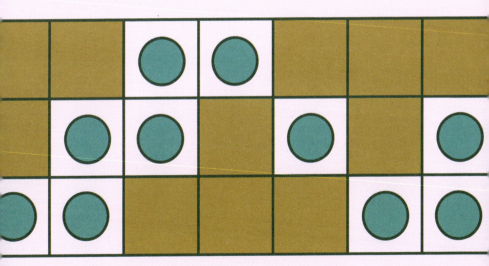

It won't be long until you start to notice that a lot of knitting involves more than one color of yarn.

Sometimes the color changes row by row. That's striped knitting.

Sometimes two colors change stitch by stitch within one row. That's stranded knitting.

And you'll see knitting where several colors appear in sections. That's intarsia.

Stripes

A row of stitches equals a stripe. This simple concept leads to infinite possibilities, varying in width, color, and texture. When you switch from one color to another when striping, you have to decide whether to: a) carry the yarn not in use up the edge of your work while you work another color, or b) cut the yarn at each color change. Mostly, it's the height of the stripe that matters. Anything more than 4 rows tall probably needs to be cut.

CARRYING YARN UP THE SIDE TO CHANGE COLORS

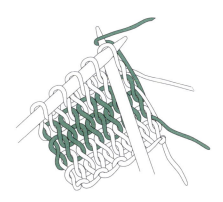

If you're knitting stripes of no more than 2 rows in one color (let's call them Color A and Color B), carry the color not in use (Color B) up the side of your work. When you get to the the end of a row and it's time for another color, simply let go of Color A and pick up Color B, lifting Color B over Color A. To keep the edge neat, don't pull the new color tightly when working the first stitch of the row.

CUTTING YARN FOR STRIPES

In cases where you are not carrying yarn up the side of the work, when it is time to change colors, cut Color A, leaving a 4" (10 cm) tail of yarn hanging. Now join Color B, leaving a 4" (10 cm) tail hanging, and begin knitting. For a refresher on how to attach a new color, see page 20.

We started this lesson by telling you that when stripes are more than 4 rows tall, you'll probably want to cut your yarn when you change colors. But to every rule there is an exception: if the edge is going to be hidden in a seam, you can often get away with carrying the yarn up the sides further than 4 rows. It's your call.

KNITTING STRIPES IN THE ROUND

Because knitting in the round creates a spiral rather than back-and-forth rows, stripes in the round require an extra bit of fussing unless you don't mind the little jog that is created at the spot where the color change happens. You'll find that the end of the stripe you just finished knitting doesn't align with its starting point. There are lots of ideas about how to fix this (if you think it's a problem) and you may go down that rabbit hole at some point, but for now we're going to invite you to embrace the jog. Lots of us do!

PRACTICING STRIPES

To get the hang of 2-row stripes, let's try them out in stockinette stitch (knit on right side rows and purl on wrong side rows).

Choose 2 colors of yarn in the same weight.

With Color A, cast on 30 stitches.

Rows 1–4: Knit 4 rows to create a stable garter-stitch border. Do not cut the yarn; let it drop for the moment.

Row 5: Join Color B. Knit this row.

Row 6: Purl using Color B. Do not cut the yarn; let it drop.

Row 7: Pick up Color A again so that it is in front of Color B. Knit this row.

Row 8: Purl using Color A. Let the yarn drop; do not cut it.

Repeat Rows 5–8 as many times as you like. Be sure to keep the yarn you're carrying up the side tidy but not tight.

To finish, knit 4 rows in Color A to make a garter-stitch border to match the beginning border. Bind off.

Stranding

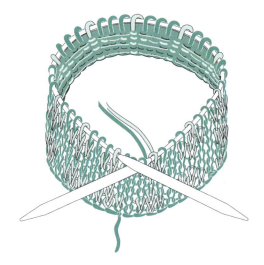

When we knit stripes, we typically work a full row or more in one color before changing to a second color. Stranded knitting is a technique that allows us to change colors every stitch or every few stitches within a row. The resulting effects are typically geometric patterns and all sorts of color play. There's a rhythm to stranded knitting, once you get the hang of it. It's one of our favorite kinds of knitting.

Note that we work stranded knitting in the round, not flat, which means the front of the work is always facing us, and we only work knit stitches (never purls). There are geniuses who knit stranded knitting flat, but we are not those geniuses.

**HOLDING TWO COLORS OF YARN
AT THE SAME TIME WHEN STRANDING**

The main challenge is knowing how to hold the yarns so that they don't tangle. The following method is one of several possible techniques: holding one color in each hand. It's the one that works well for us.

After you work this method for a while, you will develop a rhythm, halting at first, but more fluid as you practice. The hand that you normally don't rely on to form the stitches is the one that will need practice. Stay cool, and remember that it is in fact connected to your body and will soon respond to your brain's commands.

The more consistent you make your motions, the more consistent your stitches will be. Try to make the same motion with each stitch. Take it slow, and soon your fingers will know what to do.

HOLDING YARN FOR STRANDED KNITTING

1. Hold the needles loosely in your hands.

Your right hand works Color A; your left hand works Color B.

Drape Color A across the top of your right index finger, front to back.

Drape Color B across the top of your left index finger, front to back.

Your thumbs and other fingers hold the needles in place.

2. To knit Color A, insert the right needle knitwise into the next stitch.

Using your right index finger, knit Color A.

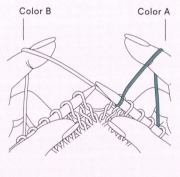

1.

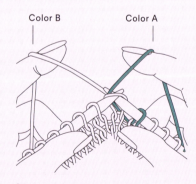

2.

3. To knit Color B, insert the right needle knitwise into the next stitch.

Using your left index finger, pull Color B so that it is somewhat snug—not too loose or tight.

Move the tip of the right needle to the right of Color B, then move it behind Color B.

Color B is now over the right needle, going from front to back. With the right needle, pull Color B through to complete a knit stitch.

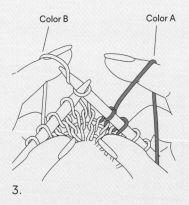

3.

WHAT'S HAPPENING ON THE BACK?

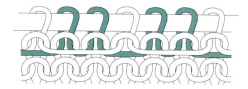

As you work a stitch pattern with more than 1 color, you will start to see horizontal lines of yarn across the back of your work. These strands need to be not too loose, not too tight. When you change to a new color of yarn, slightly spread apart the stitches on your right needle as you bring the new color behind them. This will create a bit of slack in the strand.

PRACTICING STRANDED KNITTING

To practice stranded knitting, you need to be working in the round. We suggest that you make a hat just like the one we presented in Lesson 4. But this time, work with 2 colors of worsted-weight wool, choosing one as your main color (color A) and another as your contrasting color (color B). When the piece measures about 1.5" (4 cm) from the cast-on edge, follow this chart for every round until you reach the crown shaping. From that point on, work in just one color to the end.

PEERIE PATTERN

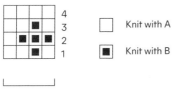

4-stitch repeat

To use this chart, start at the lower right corner. Working right to left, knit each stitch in the color shown. Repeat the pattern until the end of the round. Begin Round 2 at the right side of chart and work the pattern until the end of the round. Repeat the 4 rounds until you reach the crown shaping.

Intarsia

Think of intarsia as paint by numbers, only with yarn. It's how you put a moose, a heart, or a geometric shape on your sweater. While stranded knitting allows you to repeat small patterns, intarsia allows you to create areas of whatever size and shape you want. In this case, however, you do not strand yarn across the back of your work; instead, you work with multiple lengths of yarn at the same time. While stranded knitting is easiest to do in the round, intarsia is worked flat. The only new skills you need to learn are how to follow an intarsia chart and how to switch from one color to another.

WORKING INTARSIA FROM A CHART

You work intarsia following a chart that assigns a color to each stitch. You follow it stitch by stitch, beginning in the lower right corner, working right to left on odd-numbered (knit) rows and left to right on even-numbered (purl) rows.

> For intarsia you need at least 2 colors of yarn. After that, the sky is the limit, as long as you're willing to work with multiple strands of yarn in each row. To do this type of knitting, we follow the technique advocated by the great intarsia master/artist Kaffe Fassett. Rather than working with full balls of yarn (or smaller bobbins wrapped with yarn as some knitters do), we cut our yarn into 1-yard (-meter) lengths and let the strands hang from our work. "Pull from the tangle," Fassett advises, which we find to be handy advice for pretty much all of life.

CHANGING COLORS IN INTARSIA

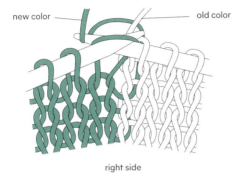

right side

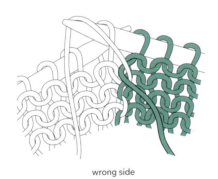

wrong side

To change colors, lay the old yarn over the new yarn before knitting the first stitch in the new yarn. Doing this will prevent a gap where the color change happens.

PRACTICING INTARSIA

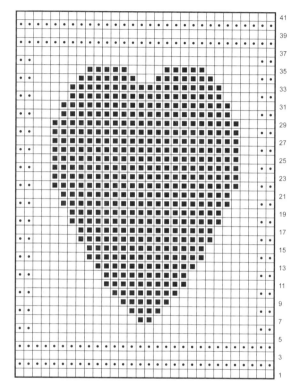

☐ Knit on right side with A, purl on wrong side with A.

⊡ Knit on wrong side with A.

■ Knit on right side with B, purl on wrong side with B.

Choose 2 colors of worsted-weight yarn. Cast on 30 stitches in Color A, and begin working from the chart above. At Row 7, you'll join a second strand of Color A, after knitting the 2 stitches of Color B. When you've completed the chart, bind off.

LESSON 7

Finishing: Weaving in Ends, Seaming, Blocking

Once you have bound off the last stitch of your project, you are likely to need to do some finishing, such as weaving in yarn tails, joining seams, and blocking using water or steam.

There's a real sense of accomplishment in assembling a project—sewing the seams, weaving in the ends. We made a whole entire complete thing. Amazing!

Weaving in Ends

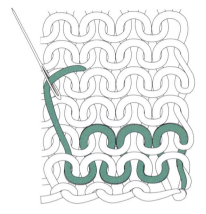

When the knitting is done, you will want to hide the ends of yarn in your work. Thread the end onto a tapestry needle. Working on the wrong side, weave the end through 6 stitches, following the shape of each stitch, then cut off the excess yarn. If you have seams in your project, weaving ends into the seams is a great way to go. If your work doesn't have any seams, then make the weaving as unobtrusive as possible. If you worked with more than 1 color, weave each end into its corresponding color section.

Seaming

Seaming is a way to connect one edge of fabric to another. For this lesson we present the 3 seaming methods that we use most: mattress stitch, backstitch, and a flat seam.

MATTRESS STITCH SEAM

Mattress stitch is magical. When you have finished sewing the seam, and you pull the seaming yarn taut, the seam is invisible from the right side of the fabric. The way you work it depends on the fabric.

MATTRESS STITCH ON STOCKINETTE SIDE-TO-SIDE

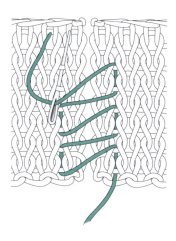

The simplest, and most common, way to use mattress stitch is to join two pieces of stockinette stitch fabric side-to-side, with the stitches going in the same direction on both pieces.

1. With right sides facing you, lay the 2 pieces edge-to-edge on a flat surface. Thread a tapestry needle with matching yarn the length of the seam plus 10" (25 cm). On one edge, insert the needle into the first row, between the edge stitch and the second stitch.

2. Take the needle under 2 rows, and bring it up to the right side. Make sure the needle comes up between the edge stitch and the second stitch of the row.

3. Take the needle to the opposite edge, insert it into the first row, between the edge stitch and the second stitch. Take it under 2 rows, and bring it to the right side.

4. Return to the first edge; insert the needle into the same hole where you brought it up. Take the needle under 2 rows and bring to the right side.

5. Return to the second edge; insert the needle into the same hole where you brought it up. Take the needle under 2 rows and bring to the right side.

6. Repeat steps 4 and 5, zigzagging back and forth between the 2 edges, always inserting the needle into the hole it came out of on the previous edge.

Every 6 stitches or so, pull on both ends of the yarn, gently but firmly, until the yarn is straight and goes tautly through the seam, and the fabric lays nice and flat.

MATTRESS STITCH ON STOCKINETTE GOING IN DIFFERENT DIRECTIONS

When using mattress stitch to join two pieces with stitches going in different directions, you follow the same principles; however, you can't go 2 stitches at a time on both sides, so it's a bit trickier to keep from stretching one edge more than the other. To avoid stretching, we recommend pinning or clipping the edges together before you start, then removing the pins or clips as you sew.

Employ trial and error until the seam looks good. One nice thing about mattress stitch is that it pulls out easily for do-overs.

MATTRESS STITCH ON GARTER STITCH

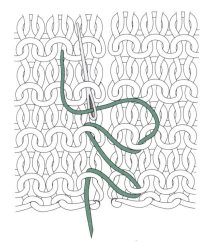

Mattress stitch for garter stitch is different; it picks up the bumps of the stitches rather than the ladder between the stitches—the "smile" on one piece (the stitch that is U-shaped) and the "frown" on the other (the upside-down U on the other piece). This keeps the garter stitch pattern working across the seam.

BACKSTITCH SEAM

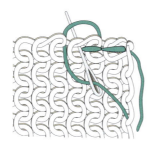

If mattress stitch won't work in a given situation, try backstitch. It is strong and flexible but bulkier than mattress stitch.

1. Backstitch is worked on the wrong side of the project. Clip fabric edges to be joined with right sides facing each other to keep them aligned and prevent stretching; remove the clips as you sew.

2. Thread a tapestry needle with a length of yarn no longer than 1 yard (meter), leaving at least a 5" (12.5 cm) tail. Bring the needle up from under the seam, through both layers, as close to the edge as possible, either a stitch or half-stitch in, and about .5" (1 cm) from the bottom of the seam.

3. Take the needle back down into the work 1 stitch behind where the needle came up.

4. Bring the needle up 1 stitch ahead of where the previous stitch began. Take the needle back down into the work where the previous stitch began.

Repeat Step 4 until the seam is complete, leaving a 5" (12.5 cm) tail at the end. Keep the tension snug but not tight.

FLAT SEAM
(ALSO KNOWN AS OVERCAST SEAM)

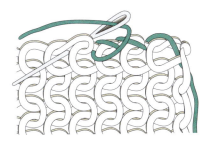

A flat seam is ideal when a seam ridge is undesirable, such as when joining a buttonhole band to a sweater body. Unlike other methods, the 2 edges of a flat seam do not overlap.

1. Place the 2 pieces together on a flat surface, with right sides facing each other. If they're identical, line up stitches and rows precisely. If the seam is longer than a few inches, clip the pieces together. Thread a length of yarn no longer than 1 yard (meter) onto a tapestry needle.

2. Leaving a tail that is at least 5" (12.5 cm) long, bring the needle up from under the seam, through both layers of the fabric, as close to the edge as possible—basically at the outermost strand of the edge—starting at the seam's very bottom.

3. Continue working as shown, keeping the stitches short and close to the edge, removing the clips as you approach them. When finished, leave a 5" (12.5 cm) tail.

Blocking

Blocking is the process of washing, shaping, and drying your finished pieces so they look their best. When your knitting looks wonky, blocking can smooth away imperfections. When your knitting looks great, it will look even better after blocking. We block everything. It's how we were raised.

1. Fill a basin with tepid water and a squirt of wool wash or shampoo. Add your handknit, and let it soak for at least 10 minutes so the fibers can absorb the water and relax. Do not agitate or lather the handknit.

2. Empty the water and squeeze as much of it out of the item as you can. Do not wring or twist the fabric.

3. Lay the wet item flat on a towel. Roll it up. Now stand on the roll. Flip it over and stand on the other side. When the towel is wet, lay the handknit flat on a dry towel. Shape it gently with your fingertips to remove any wrinkles and smooth it all out. Do not stretch it. Leave it to dry.

This is all that is needed for most handknits. Sometimes—with a lace shawl, for example—you will want to stretch the handknit and pin it out to dry. Other times, you will want to make sure your piece of knitting is a precise size, so use a tape measure or a blocking mat with a grid on it, and gently shape the knit to the correct measurements before letting it dry. But for most knitting, simply washing and letting it dry flat will work wonders.

LESSON 8

Patterns, Yarn, and Gear

A well-written pattern. Lovely yarn. A kit of handy tools. These are all part of the fun of knitting. We have a feeling you will soon want to set yourself up with good gear.

Knitting Patterns

A knitting pattern is your roadmap. A good one will tell you everything you need to have and know and do to get from start to finish.

SOURCING PATTERNS

Knitting patterns are everywhere: on the internet, on the MDK website and in our Field Guides, in books, at yarn shops. Some are free, and some are paid. We like paid patterns because the modest cost of the pattern usually goes to support a creative person, and that's always a great thing to do.

The website Ravelry.com serves as the Library of Congress for knitting patterns: hundreds of thousands of patterns are reviewed, discussed, dissected, and sold there. If you want to know what other people think of a pattern you are considering, or if you have a question about it, check out the Ravelry conversation.

PRINTED VS. DIGITAL PATTERNS

We are big believers in working from a printed pattern rather than a digital version. It's easy to carry with you. No batteries required. And you can make notes on it easily. A digital version can be handy to have as a backup, of course.

Reading a Pattern

Always read through a pattern before you begin knitting. If something seems unclear, you'll want to sort it out before you cast on. Heed our advice! We learned this the hard way!

A typical knitting pattern features these components.

Measurements
The size of the finished project—after it has been completed, washed, and blocked (see page 78).

Schematic
This drawing shows you the basic construction of your project, including measurements for all of the sizes. It helps you envision how the different parts come together. We also use it to check our measurements as we go.

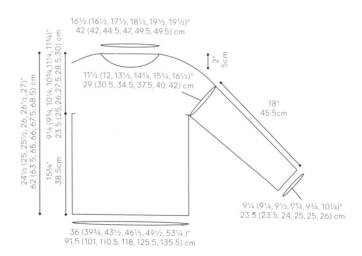

Materials
Yarn, needles, stitch markers, and any special tools or notions, such as a cable needle or buttons.

Gauge
The number of stitches and rows per inch to make the project as envisioned by the designer and to match the measurements given in the schematic. See page 90 for more on this important topic.

Notes
This is where the designer puts information they want to call your attention to before you begin knitting, such as details about the yarn, construction, and stitch patterns.

Stitch Patterns
If there are special stitch patterns used in the project (like cables or lace), they are usually spelled out here. Sometimes they include charts.

Charts
Charts provide a graphic way to visualize and follow stitch patterns.

Directions
This is where you begin knitting. Row by row, the directions tell you what to do.

Abbreviations
Patterns are typically written in an economical style full of abbreviations. A key almost always appears with the pattern. We've listed the most common ones on page 84.

COMMON ABBREVIATIONS

K	Knit
P	Purl
CO	Cast on
BO	Bind off
Beg	Begin(ning)(s)
Cn	Cable needle
Dpns	Double-pointed needles
Dec	Decrease
Inc	Increase
K2tog	Knit 2 stitches together
Kfb	Knit into the front and back of the next stitch.
P2tog	Purl 2 stitches together
Pm	Place marker
Rep	Repeat(ed)(ing)(s)
RS	Right Side
Rnd(s)	Round(s)
Sl	Slip
Sm	Slip marker
Ssk	Slip 1 stitch knitwise, slip 1 stitch purlwise, insert left needle into front of these 2 stitches and knit together from this position.
St(s)	Stitch(es)
St st	Stockinette stitch
Tog	Together
WS	Wrong side
Wyib	With yarn in back
Wyif	With yarn in front
Yo	Yarnover

MARKING UP PATTERNS

A pattern is a working document, and we are big believers in marking it up with notes that make it easy for us to keep track of what we're doing; this will help us if we want to make the same project again. (A hundred years from now, your descendants will discover your marked-up patterns and feel tender about you. They're part of your legacy!)

Here are the two main ways we mark our patterns.

Mark your size. Knitting patterns are typically written for multiple sizes, so we always circle the numbers related to the size we're making, from start to finish, then we go back to double-check that we circled the right ones.

Write out repeats. Instructions often tell us to repeat a group of rows a specific number of times. Or sometimes an entire section will be repeated. So, when the pattern says, "Repeat 8 times," we write out 1, 2, 3, 4, 5, 6, 7, 8 and cross them off, one by one, as we complete them. This may sound a bit too literal, but we like knowing we're on track.

ERRATA

Mistakes happen. Save yourself frustration by checking the pattern page on Ravelry.com before you begin. You may also find corrections on the designer's or publisher's website.

Choosing Yarn

At the beginning of your knitting adventure, yarn is just yarn. That's why at the start of this book, we simply told you which type of yarn and needles to pick up. We wanted you to be able to cast on and go straightaway.

Quickly, though, you'll learn two important lessons: 1) The hunt for the perfect yarn for a project is one of the many pleasures of knitting; and 2) yarns vary—a lot—and these variations make a difference. The most significant variables are fiber (i.e., wool, alpaca, cotton, linen, acrylic) and thickness (sometimes called weight).

If you choose a yarn that is the wrong fiber for a project—such as cotton for a hat that you want to be snug and warm—you'll be disappointed. If you choose a yarn that is the wrong weight, your end result will not be the intended size.

As a beginner, you'll want to glean as much information as possible from the yarn label.

Reading a Yarn Label

Yarn labels convey a lot of information that will help you decide whether the yarn is right for your project, and they convey it using specific terminology, which we'll demystify for you here.

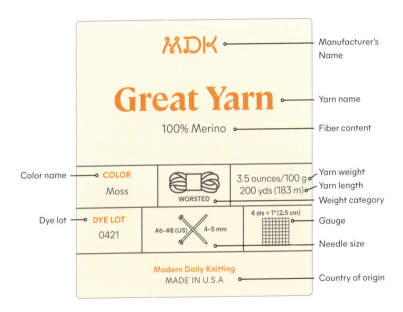

FIBER CONTENT

Yarn can be made from animal, plant, or synthetic fibers, or from a blend of fibers.

Animal Fibers: The most common animal fiber for knitting is sheep's wool. Different breeds produce wool with varying characteristics such as softness, springiness, and durability. Wool is warm (even when wet), lightweight, and takes dye beautifully. Other animal fibers come from goats (which can produce cashmere or mohair), alpacas, yaks, rabbits (which produce angora), llamas, camels, musk oxen, and silkworms.

Plant-Based Fibers: The most common plant-based yarns are cotton and linen. Some new yarns are made out of cellulose extracted from other plants, including bamboo, corn, and seaweed. Plant fibers are cool, breathable, and great for wearing in warm weather. While plant-based yarns generally lack the springiness that is prized in wool, there is a beautiful tradeoff: fabrics knit from plant-based yarns, particularly linen and cellulose, have a beautiful drape—they swing instead of cling.

Blends: Sometimes different fibers are blended together with brilliant results. Blending cotton with wool, for example, makes the cotton springier and the wool cooler to wear.

Synthetics: Synthetic fibers, such as acrylic, are manufactured from petroleum products. Projects made with them are long-lasting (though they may pill) and machine-washable.

YARN STATS

The label will tell you how much the yarn weighs and measures. The thicker the yarn, the fewer yards/meters there will be in a unit of weight. The thinner the yarn, the more yards/meters there will be in a unit of weight. A thin yarn generally knits into a very lightweight, fine fabric, with small stitches. A thick yarn generally knits into a heavier fabric, with larger stitches. It's a simple matter of physics: a very thick yarn can't be compressed into very small stitches.

When knitters discuss yarn, they use traditional names for the different weights. Here are the common ones, from thin to thick (otherwise known as light to heavy).

Lace: for shawls and transparent garments like veils

Fingering: most commonly used for socks and gloves

Sport and DK: lightweight sweaters and baby garments

Worsted, Aran, and Chunky: heavier sweaters, hats, mittens, and scarves

Bulky and Super Bulky: hats and scarves and even sweaters, and also for home items like rugs and cushions

Can you knit a sweater with fingering-weight yarn? Yes, you can, and knitters often do. These traditional weights are just a frame of reference.

NEEDLE SIZE

Needles are labeled by their US size (from 000 to 17, 35, or even 50) and by their diameter as measured in millimeters. Example: A US size 6 needle is 4 millimeters in diameter.

The yarn label will recommend a needle size, or a range of needle sizes, appropriate for that yarn to be knitted to a fabric of the recommended gauge.

The general principle: To knit a thin yarn, use a thin needle. To knit a thick yarn, use a thick needle.

RECOMMENDED GAUGE

Gauge is how knitters specify how loose or dense a fabric is: it's the number of stitches per inch or centimeter. We could call a knitted fabric thick, thin, fine, or coarse, but those words are subjective, and relative. Thin compared to what?

Typically a fingering-weight yarn is labeled as having a recommended gauge of between 7 and 8 stitches per inch (2.5 cm). A worsted-weight yarn label recommends a gauge of between 4 and 5 stitches per inch (2.5 cm). A super bulky yarn label recommends a gauge of just 1.5 or 2 stitches per inch (2.5 cm)—which is a very big stitch.

On a yarn label you will see the gauge that the yarn company thinks will produce a nice fabric in stockinette stitch. Your knitting pattern may suggest a different gauge for the same yarn.

HOW TO SWATCH AND MEASURE YOUR GAUGE

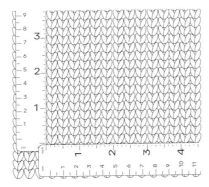

Every knitter is unique. Two knitters (let's say you and the designer of the pattern you want to make) will often achieve different gauges with the same yarn and needle size. That's why we have to swatch.

To get an accurate measurement over 4" (10 cm), which is commonly the area over which gauge is measured, make a swatch about 5" (12.5 cm) wide and tall. Begin by casting on enough stitches (with worsted-weight yarn, that will probably be about 25 stitches). Knit at least 5" (12.5 cm) in your stitch pattern and bind off. Wash and dry your swatch as you intend to wash and dry the finished piece.

Lay the swatch on a flat surface and measure in the center. You can use a ruler, but knitters often use a tool called a gauge check; it has a cut-out window, making it easier to count stitches and rows.

Count the number of stitches and rows in the center 4" (10 cm).

If the gauge you are measuring matches what is called for in the pattern, you're good to go. If you have more stitches per unit than the recommended gauge, you are knitting too tight. You need to try again with a larger needle. If you have fewer stitches per unit than the recommended gauge, you are knitting too loose. You need to try again with a smaller needle.

KNITTING TO GAUGE

Sometimes we are able to match the pattern's stitch gauge but not the row gauge; if we can't hit both perfectly, then we match the stitch gauge and just get as close as possible to the row gauge and adapt how many rows we knit to compensate. That's where the measurements on the schematic (see page 82) really help.

Swatching is a trial-and-error approach. It takes time, but if the size of your finished piece matters, it's time well spent.

But what if the size of your finished piece doesn't matter? Then, my friend, we grant you permission to skip swatching if you so choose. For blankets, scarves, dishcloths and similar items, as long as we feel that the fabric we're knitting looks and feels the way we want it to, we generally don't worry too much about gauge.

COLOR NAME/NUMBER AND DYE LOT

Yarn companies typically give each color of yarn a name and/or number. For example, you might find a yarn identified as Merlot 40 or Cornflower 23. In addition to the color number and name, you will see a dye lot. All of the yarn in the same dye lot was dyed together at the same time, which means it ought to be an exact (or very close to exact) match. When you buy multiple balls of yarn for a single project, make sure it all comes from the same dye lot.

Hand-dyed yarns typically do not have dye lots. The color in some hand-dyed yarns will vary from batch to batch, so always try to buy enough yarn for your project from the start rather than thinking you can go back to the dyer for more yarn later.

CARE INSTRUCTIONS

Yarn labels typically give care instructions. Some wool and wool-blend yarns, called superwash yarns, are treated so that they can be machine-washed and -dried without shrinking. Many synthetic yarns are also labeled as machine washable.

Our advice: All handknits look better and last longer if they are hand-washed in tepid water, squeezed gently until damp, and laid out on a flat surface to air dry. It's not a lot of trouble, and it feels good to take care of something you spent time making by hand.

Gear

We started this book by telling you that all you need is a set of needles and a ball of yarn and you are ready to knit. That is true. But it's also true that good tools can make knitting even more fun.

Our essential knitting tool kit contains the items listed below. Beyond these, we support any and all gizmos, knicknacks, and tools that make you happy.

A set of interchangeable needles
These sets include pairs of needle tips in a range of sizes from small to large and cables of varied lengths. The tips either snap or screw onto the cables. These are a significant investment, but they're a big help and save time and money in the long run.

Needle sizer
This flat tool has holes for checking your needle size. Never assume you know what size needle you're using.

Good scissors
A cute pair of sharp scissors makes cutting yarn a bit more fun.

Crochet hook
This is a crucial aid when fixing dropped stitches. You'll want a few different sizes to accommodate different weights of yarn.

5.00 mm

Stitch holders
Certain projects require you to hold live stitches while you work another section. Stitch holders look like big safety pins. If we have a ton of stitches to hold, we use yarn rather than a stitch holder. Using a tapestry needle, thread some waste yarn through all the stitches, removing the knitting needle as you go.

Stitch markers
There is a huge universe of these little guys: metal or plastic, plain or decorative. Locking stitch markers attach to fabric and solid circles slip onto needles.

Row counter
This gadget lets you click off the rows as you complete them so you can keep track of instructions like "decrease every 10th row."

Cable needle (cn)
This tool gives you a place to hold stitches to the front or back when you are working cables. It is made in a few different shapes; they all work well. If you don't have one, you can use a double-pointed needle. Or a swizzle stick.

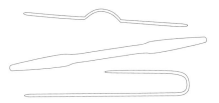

Tapestry (yarn) needles
These blunt-tipped needles with large eyes for yarn are essential for seams and weaving in ends.

Clips
To hold pieces of knitting together when we're seaming, we use pins, clothespins, or even pincer-style hair clips.

Retractable tape measure
Always measure your work on a flat surface.

LESSON 9

Fixing Mistakes

Mistakes are an inevitable part of knitting. We all make them, all the time. The good news is that they're almost always fixable with a bit of time and patience. And when we don't feel patient, we can just move on to another project and come back to the problem when we feel ready, perhaps after a good night's sleep and a cup of coffee.

Dropped Stitches

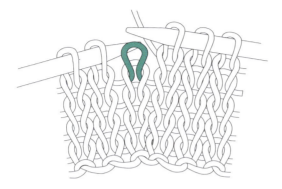

In knitting, when a stitch that is supposed to be on our needles is no longer there, we call it a dropped stitch. Everybody drops stitches. They bop off your needle when you're not watching, or when you are watching but aim your needle wrong. Or when you put your knitting down then pick it up later and discover that you've dropped a stitch and you have no idea how. You must always fix a dropped stitch. If you don't, it can unravel all the way down to your cast-on edge.

The dropped stitch looks like a loop unattached to anything above it. It can be one row down or several. Or a hundred. (Ask us how we know this.)

PICKING UP A DROPPED STITCH ONE ROW DOWN

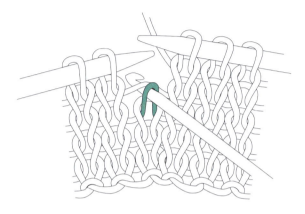

Recovering a dropped stitch

When you notice a dropped stitch in your knitting, catch it so it can't unravel any further. Use whatever you can to secure it—a locking stitch marker, paper clip, safety pin, even a piece of string threaded through the stitch.

Next, recover the dropped stitch. The goal here is to rework the dropped stitch by making a chain of interlocking stitches, as follows:

1. Knit to the point where the dropped stitch is between the 2 needles. Lay your work on a table with the front of the fabric facing you. Insert the crochet hook into the dropped stitch, front to back. With the hook, catch the yarn in the row above, and pull it through the dropped stitch to make a new stitch.

2. Slip the recovered stitch back onto the left needle, making sure that it is mounted so that the right side of the stitch is in the front of the needle (see page 28 for more on stitch mount). Recommence knitting as usual.

> Knitting allows you the chance to achieve perfection. Or not. We are not perfectionists. If we discover a missed decrease 20 rows ago, we are likely to let it go. A lot of mistakes don't matter. But dropped stitches do matter and need to be fixed.

PICKING UP A DROPPED STITCH SEVERAL ROWS DOWN

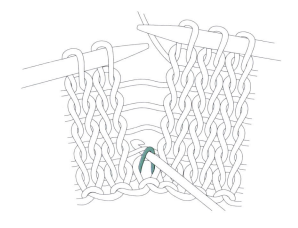

Sometimes you won't realize you've dropped a stitch until you're a few or many rows beyond it. No need to worry. Just knit or unknit to the point where the dropped stitch is between the two needles; it will look like a ladder with the dropped stitch waiting for rescue at the bottom. Insert your crochet hook into it, and pick up each rung of the ladder in order, making your way all the way to the top and positioning the final picked-up stitch on your left needle.

Recovering from a Needle Blowout

You will, at some point, accidentally drop a needle out of a work in progress, look with horror at a row or round of vulnerable live stitches, and feel desperate to save them. It might happen when you are pulling your project out of your bag (you'll be more careful next time) or when your project slips from your hands onto the floor. Or maybe you'll leave your knitting on the couch and your dog will grab it and make a run for it. Whatever the circumstances, focus on getting all those stitches back on the needles as gently as possible to keep the loose stitches from unraveling.

Place your knitting in a stable location, such as on a table. Ease each stitch back onto the needle, not worrying about whether it is mounted correctly. Just catch everything you can. When you start knitting again, you will be able to adjust the stitch mount as needed (see page 28). When you are finished, count the stitches on your needle to make sure you have all of them. If your number is off, then examine your work carefully to figure out where you might have missed a stitch, and go back and get it.

Undoing Your Knitting

At some point you'll want to undo your knitting, that is, take away stitches already completed. Maybe you need to get back to a missed decrease you just noticed, a stitch pattern isn't working, or you worked an extra row before a cable cross. There are basically two ways of doing this: ripping and unknitting.

RIPPING

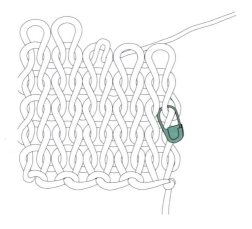

The fastest way to bid farewell to knitting you don't like is to mark the row you want to get back to with a stitch marker, and start unraveling, pulling the yarn gently out of the stitches. The goal is to undo your knitting without disturbing the stitches you want to preserve. Then put all of the live preserved stitches back on the needle in the correct orientation (see page 28). Go slowly and double-check your work.

UNKNITTING

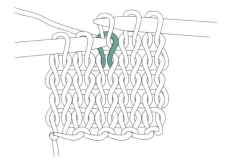

To unknit (or "tink," a word that is literally "knit" backwards), you remove stitches one at a time. This can be a slow process, but it gives you a lot of control. It's best used for lace, complex stitch patterns, or yarns that are slippery.

As you unknit, watch out for decreases and increases, cables, and yarnovers—you will need to work back carefully when you arrive at these. This is not fast work, but it is the safest way to preserve a stitch pattern.

Put the tip of your left needle into the stitch below the stitch on the right needle, then let the stitch above pull out and drop away. Collect stitches on your left needle as you tink your way across the right needle.

> Another option for undoing: ask a friend who knows what they're doing to do it for you and spare yourself the sight of your work unraveling.

What we haven't taught you

What's next?

So very much.

Everything in this book is designed to get you started, but we know from our own experience that getting started doesn't take very long. You have so much to look forward to: Casting on for that first sweater. Knitting far into the night. Waking up and knitting before you even get out of bed. Trying out new yarns and techniques and deciding which ones you love most. Diving into a pattern that looks a little too complicated at first, then figuring it all out. Attending your first fiber festival. We are decades into this thing called knitting and, amazingly, we haven't explored it all—or even come close.

Most of all, you have a community of knitters to meet, a community that stretches around the globe. The two of us became friends on the internet—it took years before we met in person—and it is how we continue to communicate daily with each other and thousands of equally passionate knitters.

We heartily invite you to join us online at Modern Daily Knitting, where we publish something new every morning. There are how-to videos and a forum where you can compare notes and spend time with other knitters who love to knit as much as you do. And we have an online shop that we stock with the yarns, tools, books, and sundries that we love.

Skill Set: Beginning Knitting

Copyright © 2021 by Modern Knitting Media, LLC

All rights reserved. No part of this book may be used or reproduced in any manner without written permission except in the case of brief quotations embodied in critical articles and reviews. For more information, write to us at moderndailyknitting.com.

Editor/Creative Director: Melanie Falick
Graphic Designer/Cover Artist: Lily Piyathaisere
Illustrator: Patti Pierce Stone
Technical Editor: Sue McCain

Printed in China.

ISBN: 978-1-7339456-6-0